Hope For My Success

Motivational Inspirations

By
PHETOLE CEDRIC MALEMELA

Copyright Phetole Cedric Malemela © 2017

Published by

William Jenkins
2503 4288 Grange Street
Burnaby BC V5H 1P2
Canada

williamhenryjenkins@gmail.com
http://williamjenkins.ca
Cell: 1-778-928-6139

Written by

Phetole Cedric Malemela

**262 Madiba Street
408 Karl Kling Building
Pretoria, 0002 South Africa
Malemelaphetolecedric580@gmail.com**

ISBN-13: 978-1-928164-20-3

ISBN-10: 192816420X

DEDICATION

To every young person who desires the best in Life:

May the principles on these pages serve as a roadmap in your life.

To every parent who wants to help their children make wise decisions.

ACKNOWLEDGMENT

No accomplishment in life is without the cooperative effort of many gifted people who willingly and passionately dedicate themselves to excellence and quality. This book is no different. All we are on this human journey to eternity is the sum total of what we have learned from those who have shared their thoughts with us. I am eternally gratefully to the many teachers through the years who have given me the information, inspiration, and revelations.

Thank you all for making me who I have become.

First, this book is the result of my own experiences and how I understand things in life. In this regard I would like to thank my dad, Malemela Sekwape Judas, my beloved mother, Malemela Selina Maruping, and my grandmother Pulane Grace Malatji who laid an excellent foundation in the Word of God for all their 4 children. I would like to thank my spiritual mother and father, Pastor Andries & Magdeline Mogoboya for the word of God and guidance .Thanks to my Sister, Kedibone Constance Pudikabekwa. She taught me a lot in Christ. To my friend Mandy Mahasha: You inspired me to go on. You have always been a source of strength and a shield of protection. You are the best! Thanks to all my friends and relatives for their support.

These principles taught me wise judgment and kept me from the many mistakes that young people encounter.

Phetole Cedric Malemela

Phetole Cedric Malemela was born in Lephepane, Tzaneen, South Africa in 1993. He is the first born of Mr. Judas and Mrs. Selina Malemela, followed by three siblings, one sister and two brothers. He reflects a varied personality including ambition and the qualities of generosity and thoughtfulness. He is also a well determined and vigorous individual, yet pleasantly calm. He encourages working hard for what you desire and believe in, and doing it through God. He knows that nothing great comes easily and that with God everything is possible.

He is motivated by his love for learning about computers and succeeding as he strives to become an outstanding and successful man in today's society with the goal of becoming a professional and well-known computer technician.

x

Table of Contents

Introductory Message 1
CHAPTER 1 MAKE IT WORK 3
CHAPTER 2 HOLD ON 7
CHAPTER 3 GROWING UP, LETTING GO AND LIVING A LIFE OF WHICH YOU ARE PROUD 9
CHAPTER 4 HOPE FOR MY SUCCESS 12
CHAPTER 5 A LOVE STORY 15
CHAPTER 6 TEMPTATIONS 18
CHAPTER 7 CURRICULUM VITAÉ 21
CHAPTER 8 SELF- LOVE 23
CHAPTER 9 DATING 26
CHAPTER 10 LIFE LESSONS 28
CHAPTER 11 RIGHT CHOICES MAKE LIFE SO MUCH BETTER 30
CHAPTER 12 MANUAL FOR LOVE 32
CHAPTER 13 BE YOURSELF 36
CHAPTER 14 GRATITUDE 38
CHAPTER 15 FAVOURITE QUOTES 40
CHAPTER 16 MAKE IT HAPPEN 42
CHAPTER 17 HONESTY AND INTEGRITY 44
CHAPTER 18 A FAMILY OF FRIENDS 46
THE COMMANDMENTS 48
About the Publisher 50

Introductory Message

Everyone has them: those days where nothing seems to get done, except maybe what you've added to your already lengthy to-do list. Are you tired most of the time? Do you find yourself wishing for a better day—a simpler day? Too many things compete for your limited resources of attention, energy, and time. You may be suffocating and not even know it. If you feel like this, you're not alone. Most people today live complicated lives that leave them frustrated and confused, weary and worn out. But I have good news: your life does not have to be that way. You can choose a life of simplicity, fruitfulness, fulfillment, peace, and joy.

Develop an ability to give yourself to what you are doing. You will sense an awareness enabling you to enjoy the current activity, instead of going through each day in a blur of activity and confusing thoughts which leave you drained and exhausted.

Do you fear you will not accomplish as much if you try to live this way? It's true you may not do as much, but you will also enjoy what you do *a whole lot more.* One key to simplicity is realizing that quality is far superior to quantity.

CHAPTER 1 MAKE IT WORK

Remember that God's Love is the ultimate. Knowing the love God has for you means that you do not have to seek fulfillment in how anyone makes you feel, the most perfect love comes from God, and it is always yours. He will do much more to fill the love-space than a person ever could. Approach your relationship knowing that God likes you and loves you, and there is plenty of room for wonders of love, marriage, mature family love. Always remember He sent His son, Jesus to die for your sins. Make sure you are strong in your loving relationship with God. This means knowing that He is always there to help you along the way. Trust Him.

My mother used to say to me "Son, dating is for adults. If you date, don't come back to my house".

Even now I know that she wants me to work first, have my own house and cars before taking a wife. I now thank God because since she taught me to take care of myself, I never disappointed her despite the fact that I didn't complete my studies.

So make God the most important part in your life.

Make Him the love of your life. Know the ideal match for you. Date someone that you would consider marrying. Choose a person that has a similar desire for God, one that will build you up in your faith. If you are already in a relationship, positively encourage one another in pursuing God. Help your boyfriend or girlfriend to keep God as your first priority. Pray about your dating relationship. Give everything over to God. Let God know that you are asking His approval. Talk to God about the problems that arise. Thank Him for the opportunity to be in a relationship and the happy times you experience. You can also pray with your boyfriend or girlfriend. It is a good way to help each other out with whatever stresses life brings.

By praying together, you are experiencing God together. Though it could make the focus more about you two building intimacy, still there is a tendency to bring out one another's faults in prayer; therefore, avoid prodding, interrogating, judging. Instead, help each other in order to build trust; love and forgive each other as the Lord's Prayer models for us. Talk about God. Make an effort to bring God into your conversations Not only will it help in keeping God on your minds, you will also find out about each other's beliefs. Talking about a spiritual subject changes normal conversation into one of eternal significance. Discussing God also allows you to build up each other's knowledge and confidence.

Read the Bible. Keeping God's words in your heart helps you to remember the love and promises He has for you. Try reading the Bible together. It could be fun, spiritual and good for conversation. Different verses will help you along the way in your relationship.

CHAPTER 2 HOLD ON

Hold on and don't let go of your dreams. Don't give up because you will make it one day. They say quitters never win and winners never quit, so I say to you "Try and if you fail, don't be shy of defeat because it takes a lot of courage to keep on moving". Just hold on and be strong because what you going through won't last long. Decide in your heart of hearts what really excites and challenges you, and start moving your life in that direction. Every decision you make, from what you eat to what you do with your time, turns you into who you are tomorrow, and the day after that.

Look at who you want to be, and start sculpting yourself into that person. You may not become exactly what you thought you would be, but you will be doing things that suit you in a profession you believe in. Don't let life randomly kick you into the adult you don't want to become. Solidifying your own legacy means you go through Hell and high water just to make your family proud and to let them know you're making a name for yourself. Failure sometimes gives you the opportunity to know and discover your hidden abilities.

I discovered my talents and interest in computers the hard way. I failed at school and failed my first year as an IT student. But no matter what, I went after my talents and now I feel good and enjoy what I do. So, failure revolves around those who progress. I do not know what the future holds, but I do know what I presently hold: Determination, Hope, and GOD. I want people to know it's not a bad thing to fail. Keep pushing until something happens.

CHAPTER 3 GROWING UP, LETTING GO AND LIVING A LIFE OF WHICH YOU ARE PROUD

As a coming-of-age adult, I am quickly learning the many setbacks life often presents. Things that once seemed perfect no longer fit into your life, and the goals you once dreamed of accomplishing have been replaced by new ones. You find yourself challenged by what you were raised to believe, enlightened by the new people you meet, and immersed in the new environment around you. Suddenly, you find yourself completely changed. Where does this leave you?

With respect to relationships, sometimes it's hard to admit when you've grown apart from someone, especially if, at one time, that person fit into your life perfectly. This person could be anyone, a friend, a family member or even a past love. Growing up has a tendency to deeply change people.

The things that propel and guide you through life are now different from those of your once best friend, which explains why you both are now moving in different directions.

As for your romantic interests, here's my advice: be unapologetic. In this period of your life, you will change and develop as a person far more than you ever will in your entire lifetime. Don't feel guilty about letting someone go who was once so important to you. People change. Value the memories you have with someone, but don't be afraid to stand alone. Don't be afraid to be your own priority.

I have long ago accepted that certain things are not, and will never be for me. I hold myself to a high standard, and I have no problem being the odd one out or being the only one not participating.

If you are ever in a situation where you feel uneasy or feel pressured to participate, please understand it's okay to say no. In today's society, and more specifically for the younger generation as a whole, many behaviors and attitudes are considered the norm, but they are by no means normal. It's not normal to go out every night and return drunk. It's not normal to irresponsibly use drugs. It's not normal to hook up with every person you're attracted to (and sometimes not attracted to). I'm not judging anyone. Live your life the way you want to if it makes you happy, but realize that the way you choose to spend your days is how you will live your life.

CHAPTER 4 HOPE FOR MY SUCCESS

Nobody is successful in any venture just by wishing they would be. Successful people make a plan and talk to themselves about that plan constantly. You can think things on purpose, and if you make what you think about match what you actually want to do, your feelings may not like it, but they will go along. We all want to be successful. Everyone has an inner desire to succeed. This desire can be strong and at times we can become very competitive. We want to run faster, jump higher and endure longer. Our goals change as we grow older and we strive to succeed in other areas of life. Some seek success in professions such as health care or business. Some become pilots or astronauts. Others become musicians or authors. But no matter what path we take in life, we all have one common factor, we want to succeed.

There is another common factor. No matter how successful we are, sometimes we feel as though we have failed! Why is that? Are there changes we can make to reduce or eliminate this feeling of failure? Actually, there are changes we can make that will set us on the course for success. While physical success in life is important, true happiness can only be achieved through spiritual success.

Our relationship with our Heavenly Father is a spiritual relationship and this is the most important area where we must succeed. This chapter is dedicated to helping people grasp spiritual concepts that touch their lives. Spiritual success is a concept that is extremely important. God wants us to be successful. Our Creator does not want us to fail or to feel like a failure. He created us with a definite purpose in mind. God wants us to have hope, to have a future, a successful future.

"For I know the thoughts that I have for you, says the Lord, thoughts of peace and not of evil, to give you a future and a hope". (Jeremia 29:11)

CHAPTER 5 A LOVE STORY

I've never been lucky in love. I always predicted the end of every relationship. I expected every single word I've been told. Every little fake emotion I thought real so far. All along this road, I was guided by an Angel, the one who protected me from harm, wiped away my tears, the one who brought this joy and happiness to my life. She was a bright angel, a shiny diamond.

Suddenly out of nowhere she became the main character of my most beautiful and painful relationship. She was the charming princess of my love story, the beast into my nightmare. Still I couldn't keep grudges against her because, above all, she was my best friend. She was the one I loved as a sister, the one who shared my secrets, just like a shadow. The beginning of the relationship was as sudden and blurry as its ending. I won't lie and say I was fine with it. It hurt deeply, but as I like to say, what doesn't kill you makes you stronger. I think this time it's much different.

We grew up, learned from our mistakes, and we do know now, unlike the first time, the risks and damage it would cause to play with each other's feelings. How do I feel after all that? Fine! I should say that it is incredible how things can change! How a single person can turn your world around. How a single person can make you cry until you bleed or make you laugh until you cry. Despite the fact that she hurt me more than anyone else, she made a sense to my dreams, gave a point to my existence. We shared my secrets, my hopes, my fears. She made me unique. I don't need a mirror to see myself anymore. I only have to look into her eyes to see the reflection of the perfect person she made of me.

There are times when neither of us can stand the other one. These times I feel we're completely disconnected.

CHAPTER 6 TEMPTATIONS

HERE'S HOW WE GET TEMPTED:
Fantasy – Flirtation – Fall.

First, we allow it to grow in our mind. Then, we began to flirt with it. Then we fall.

You need to deal with temptation at the early stage of fantasy. That way, if you stumble, you can still pull back. You have to watch over your heart with all diligence. You have to respect your body as it is written in the bible that our bodies are the Temple of God. You have to be careful where you go, who you associate with and what you watch, because you have a responsibility to watch over your heart.

HERE ARE TWO SIMPLE STEPS THAT HELPED ME:

Repent and know who you are in Christ

Repent

To repent is to change how you think. When you try to take a shortcut to change on the outside, you'll never be able to change. Romans 12:1-2 says Be transformed by the changing of your mind. It's your thought life. As I got my mind renewed, my desires changed.

You're not going to be able to use your strong will to do it. Addictions can be delivered instantly, but sometimes it's just that you need your mind renewed. It's like a pig: you can dress him up, make him look good, but when he sees mud, he's going to jump in. Why? It's because he's not changed on the inside.

Know who you are in Christ
These scriptures will help you know what you have now that you are in the family of God. Confess these scriptures. As you get these in your heart, your desires will change, and as a result your actions will change.

I thank God that comparatively early in my life he opened my eyes to see what the devil could do; then he showed me my responsibility and what I could do as a "new creature" in Christ Jesus by resisting the devil. I feel that I owe my life to the use of his truth. I have been sorely tempted, terribly harassed, and driven to despair, feeling helpless, hopeless, and abandoned of God; but by his Grace I have risen again and again in the name of the Lord and resisted the Devil.
I was tempted and tried by the Devil

CHAPTER 7 CURRICULUM VITAÉ

Name: JESUS CHRIST
Address: Ephesians 1:20
Phone: Romans 10:13
Website: Bible

QUALIFICATIONS

I founded the earth and established the heavens, (See Proverbs 3:19)
I formed man from the dust of the ground, (See Genesis 2:7)
I breathed into man the breath of life, (See Genesis 2:7)

EDUCATIONAL BACKGROUND

I can even tell you all of the secrets of your heart, (See Psalms 44:21).

SKILLS AND WORK EXPERIENCES

I am a Wonderful Counselor, (See Isaiah 9:6). People who listen to me shall dwell safely and shall not fear evil, (See Proverbs 1:33). Most importantly, I have the authority, ability and power to cleanse you of your sins, (See 1 John 1:7-9)

MAJOR ACCOMPLISHMENTS

I was an active participant in the greatest Summit Meeting of all times, (See Genesis 1:26). I laid down my life so that you may live, (See II Corinthians 5:15).

REFERENCES

Believers and followers worldwide will testify to my divine healings, salvation, deliverance, miracles, restoration and supernatural guidance.

CHAPTER 8 SELF-LOVE

A whole person is one who has, first of all, a healthy self-concept. Many people struggle with feelings of inferiority and self-hatred. Such persons will have problems in any relationship. Healthy self-love is critically important to personal wholeness because it affects every other relationship.

I finally developed the courage to move on after the break up with the woman I loved with my whole heart. I had to live with the effects of lack of self-love. I struggled to eat, sleep, or continue my daily functioning. I spent every waking hour to myself, trying to understand how and why I had gotten there. I had to know, because whatever it was, if I did not attend to it, this was going to be the end of the road for me. I knew it.

I watched "The Notebook" movie five more times, cried, and phoned a friend to keep me company while I ate my few bites each day. During this whole time, I found places in my story where I was not present to my own life, my body or my spirit. I was just there. I found the places where I had abandoned myself and then became angry at the other person for hurting me. The truth was, I did not have a big enough inner container to hold the love I so desired even if I received it, because my self-love tank had shrunk down to the size of a bottle cap.

It finally became very clear to me that there was one core reason I had arrived there: I did not know anything about self-love. This realization launched me into a relentless search for the meaning of self-love, internally and externally. I found that self-love is a not a destination; it's a practice. Self-love is the foundation on which we build a happy life. Without self-love, we have nowhere to put the love or abundance that comes to us.

Someone once asked Jesus what was the greatest commandment of all.

Jesus replied: "'Love the Lord your God with all your heart and with all your soul and with all your mind.' This is the first and greatest commandment. And the second is like it: 'Love your neighbor as yourself.' All the Law and the Prophets hang on these two commandments" (Matt. 22:37-40).

So, I say love unconditionally.

CHAPTER 9 DATING

You are ready to date when you have first learned how to be single. Learn to be an asset first. You should be preoccupied with preparing yourself for whomever God is preparing for you. Most people are so busy looking for the one God has prepared for them that they fail to prepare themselves for that person. I always say to my friends, "Don't marry your lover, marry your friend," because physical and emotional love are 100 percent chemical.

If you marry your lover, you are basing your marriage on chemical reactions, which change like the weather.

When you date, focus on the spiritual instead of the physical. Use your dating time not to groom a lover but to grow a friend. The more you walk, talk, and behave consistent with your highest values, the more you will like yourself and the better you will feel about yourself. Your self-image will improve and your level of self-acceptance will go up. You will feel stronger, bolder, and more capable of facing any challenge.

MY WISHES FOR YOU...

Where there is pain, I wish you peace and mercy.

Where there is self-doubting, I wish you a renewed confidence in your ability to work through it.

Where there is tiredness, or exhaustion, I wish you understanding, patience, and renewed strength.

Where there is fear, I wish you love, and courage.

CHAPTER 10 LIFE LESSONS

There are many things in life that I have discovered. Some of them are the things I went through, some I'm still going through.

I have realized that there is a role for everyone you meet in life. Some will test you, some will use you, some will love you, and some will teach you. The ones that are important are the ones who bring out the best in you. They are the rare and amazing people who remind you why life is worth it. It's funny how people can change. One day you mean everything to them, and the next day they treat you like you do not even exist. In life, you got to learn to walk away from people and situations that threaten your peace of mind, self-respect, or your self-worth.

There are things in life that we don't want to happen, but have to accept, things we don't know, but have to learn. So whenever you're in pain, know that God wants you to win and overcome whatever you are going through.

God's purposes should saturate and overflow a man's life.

CHAPTER 11 RIGHT CHOICES MAKE LIFE SO MUCH BETTER

The wrong decision at the wrong time = disaster.
The wrong decision at the right time = mistake.
The right decision at the wrong time = unacceptance.
The right decision at the right time = success.

For you to achieve your full potential, you must contribute the greatest amount of value possible. You must concentrate all your energies on doing certain specialized tasks in an excellent fashion so that you can be paid the amount you want to earn and you can move ahead at the rate you want to move ahead. In order for you to specialize and do what you are best at, and more of it, you must delegate, relegate and outsource virtually everything else. You can become a superior human being by consciously acting exactly as the kind of person that you would most like to become. If you behave as an individual of integrity, courage, resolution, persistence and character, you will soon create within yourself the mental structure and habits of such a person. Your actions will become your reality. You will create a personality that is consistent with your highest aspirations.

CHAPTER 12 MANUAL FOR LOVE

So, how do you make a relationship work? How do you hold it together in the long term, through thick and thin, for better or worse, in sickness and in health, etc.? And are there ways to make it even better, the longer you are together? I wish I had been given one. I wish we all had been handed a Manual for Love in a class in high school, and taken levels two and three in college. For there are basic laws and practices we could have learned that would have made the path of intimate relationship so much easier had we only been given the proper roadmap.

I don't believe that there's one manual that would apply to every aspect of every relationship. That would be like saying there's one parenting book that applies to all parent-child configurations and would resolve every child-raising difficulty. It sounds attractive, but when that promise is made, I turn the other way, as relationships of all kinds are far too complicated to be simplified into a one-size-fits-all formula. What I have learned over many years of being in intimate relationships and guiding others through them is that there is a basic set of information and actions that can dramatically improve the daily tenor of the heart and the atmosphere in the home. For the rest of us, however, we need the manual. We need the love laws and loving actions spelled out for us so that we can learn, follow, and practice daily a language that will help us open our hearts and continually cultivate more love and attraction. This is how new, loving habits are formed. And the good news is that they can be formed! Even if you grew up without any positive role-modelling regarding love, you can still learn the actions that create loving relationships. And even if you did breathe in the benefits of witnessing a healthy marriage growing up, there's always more to learn. Fear has a sneaky way of undoing the healthy patterning, so that when your partner dips into the inner folds of your heart, fear will put up its walls and cause a sort of amnesia about the ways of love

People often say to me, "But I grew up seeing healthy marriages. I have been bullied by peers, called by names that hypnotized me into things I ended up regretting. I have been hurt by early partners. And without a doubt I absorbed false information about love, romance, attraction, and marriage through popular culture and other sources. Mostly I'm scared because part of the human condition is to learn how to navigate fear and choose love, meaning that fear is simply part of being human. Some would say that that challenges at the core of the spiritual path, and that intimate relationships are an accelerated course in learning about fear, resistance, and the walls that prevent us from loving fully. The more we can name the fear and learn the actions that break down its walls, the more we can open the chambers of the heart that let love in. And this is what needs to be included in the manual nobody received.

CHAPTER 13 BE YOURSELF

Do whatever makes you happy and stop copying other people. Be who God says you should be and be what God says you are. You need to love because love is the most powerful force in life. Set goals hoping that someday you will achieve whatever you wish to achieve. Always remember that the worst thing to be without is hope. The most destructive habit in life is worry, the worthless emotion of feeling pity for yourself and undermining yourself will get you nowhere.

Cherish and be grateful for the little things you have. Wake up and start working on building your better future than worrying. I always say these are the two most power-filled words "I CAN", even when I see that I'm failing. Beware of people who'll try and convince you to give up on your character, saying that nobody's perfect, and taunting you for being such an idealist.

The fact that nobody's perfect doesn't mean violating what you believe is right. It's good to learn from our mistakes, but we don't always need to make mistakes in order to learn. Remember that striving to be perfect and being perfect are two different ideas. Your character is unique. It may not match with anybody else. So do not try for it. Build it on the basis of your own natural abilities and inner light within you. Self-assessment, self-evaluation, introspection etc. work well, but never get disheartened by petty failures and criticism revolving around failures. Stand firm on your convictions. You are bound to succeed.

CHAPTER 14 GRATITUDE

The Lord wants you to have a spirit of gratitude in all you do and say. Live with a spirit of thanksgiving and you will have greater happiness and satisfaction in life. Gratitude will turn your heart to the Lord and help you recognize his influence and blessings in your life. Even in your most difficult times, you can find much to be grateful for. Doing so will strengthen and bless. . Gratitude unfolds the goodness of life. It turns what we have into enough, and more. It turns denial into acceptance, chaos into order, and confusion to clarity. It can turn a meal into a feast, a house into a home. Gratitude makes sense of our past, brings peace for today, and create a vision for tomorrow.

In your prayers, pour out your heart to your Father in heaven in thanks for the blessings you have received. Be specific in thanking him for his goodness, for your family, for friends, for leaders and teachers, for the Gospel, and for this Son, Jesus Christ. Express gratitude to the Lord by the way you live. When you keep his commandments and serve others, you show that that you love him and are grateful to him. Express your gratitude to others for the many ways they bless your life. (Luke 17:12-19)

CHAPTER 15 FAVOURITE QUOTES

- Happiness is to love and to be loved.
- We need to know ourselves. To understand others better.
- Life is like a sugar cane. Hard but sweet
- The best gift you can give to yourself is challenging yourself.
- Success is not about earning, it's not about status. Success is about having freedom to follow your passion. It's about living your dreams .it's about waking in the morning and say I'm born again.
- If you want to be a winner, hang around with winners.
- Sometimes, things happen to us we can't comprehend. We hurt, we cry, and we experience pain that pinches and bites our hearts and makes us cold. But the thing is that it always gets better and

better. It's just about appreciating the good times more than the bad times.
- ❖ Procrastination is the enemy of success
- ❖ Don't try to fit in, try to be unique.
- ❖ Overthinking leads to negative thoughts.
- ❖ Enjoy your youth. You'll never be younger than you are at this very moment.
- ❖ We are what we repeatedly DO.

CHAPTER 16 MAKE IT HAPPEN

It matters not how people around see you. It doesn't matter how rich or poor is your family. The only thing that matters is how you value yourself. Hope for the best and never forget that anything is possible as long as you remain dedicated to the task. Never forget to have fun along the way. Success means nothing without happiness. Share your talents, skills, knowledge, and time with others. Everything that you invest in others will return to you many times over. As I always tell my friends that never stop dreaming even if you see things are not going well.

Have faith and believe in yourself that you will conquer and reach your dreams. Even when your dreams seem impossible to reach, try anyway. You'll be amazed by what you can accomplish. I didn't complete my studies because I have failed, but because of the desires I have of reaching my destiny. I never stopped dreaming about owning my own computer repairs shop. So go out and make it happen even if it seems impossible. Turn your passion for something into profession because it takes faith and courage for things to happen. For the bible says every good gift is from above. (James.1:17)

CHAPTER 17 HONESTY AND INTEGRITY

Be honest with yourself, others, and God at all times. Being honest means choosing not to lie, steal, cheat, or deceive in any way. When you are honest, you build strength of character that will allow you to be of great service to God and others. Dishonesty harms you and others as well. If you lie, cheat, or shoplift, you damage your spirit and your relationships with others.

Being honest will enhance your future opportunities and ability to be guided by the Holy Ghost. Be honest at school; choose not to cheat in any way. Closely associated honesty is integrity. Integrity means thinking and doing what is right at all times, no matter what the consequences. When you have integrity, you are willing to live by your standards and beliefs even when no one is watching. Choose to live so that your thoughts and behavior are always in harmony with the Gospel.

He who hesitates is lost.

CHAPTER 18 A FAMILY OF FRIENDS

I create a family of friends whom I can share my hopes, dreams, sorrows, and happiness with. I ask for advices and help from family and friends. Sharing my ideas with them makes it easy for me to make a change. Since from my childhood I have made mistakes which taught me many things about living a healthy lifestyle.

People often ask me how I manage living the life I live because almost all of my friends from primary and high school are drinking alcohol and some smoke cigarettes and I don't. Would tell them it is only the grace and love of God. Do all in the name of the Lord Jesus, (Col.3:17). Be grateful for the things you can do because there are many people who wish they can be like you. In everything, give thanks to the most high God (1Thess.5:18). I am unique and so are you. Use your talent and make a world a better place. Be the change you want to see.

THE COMMANDMENTS

The Two Great Commandments

Thou shalt love the Lord thy God will thy heart, and with all thy soul, and with all thy mind. This is the first great commandment.

And the second is like unto it, thou shalt love thy neighbor as thyself. (Matthew 22:37-40)

The Ten Commandments
1. Thou shall not have other gods before me.
2. Thou shall not make for yourself a carved image.
3. Thou shall not take the name of the Lord thy God in vain.
4. Remember the Sabbath day, to keep it holy.
5. Honor thy father and thy mother.
6. Thou shalt not kill.
7. Thou shalt not commit adultery.

8. Thou shalt not steal.
9. Thou shalt not bear false witness against thy neighbor.
10. Thou shalt not covet.

(Exodus 20:3-4, 7-8, 12-17)

About the Publisher

William Jenkins is a retired computer guy who took up writing mystery-adventure stories for middle school children, age 9 to 12. By self-publishing the eight stories using Amazon's Createspace system, he became familiar with the ease of publishing and has now published ten other books for friends and relatives.

William was contacted by Jackie Mukhawana, a secondary school student in Tzaneen, South Africa and together they produced an anthology of plays, stories and poems written by Jackie and his friends.

If you happen across this publication and are interested in having your writing published, send a sample of the writing to the publisher using email address williamhenryjenkins@gmail.com. There is no charge for this service.

www.ingramcontent.com/pod-product-compliance
Lightning Source LLC
Chambersburg PA
CBHW060857050426
42453CB00008B/999